PAUL

THIRTEENTH APOSTLE

15 Studies for Individuals or Groups

CHUCK & WINNIE CHRISTENSEN

Harold Shaw Publishers • Wheaton, Illinois

CONTENTS

INTRODUCTION

The apostle Paul ranks with the great world-changers of all time. After a dramatic conversion experience, the former persecutor of Christians became a devoted follower of Christ. He traveled, preached, and wrote with unfailing energy. Being a Jew who was raised in the Roman world made Paul especially well suited to minister to both Jews and Gentiles. He received the finest education of his time and was able to speak convincingly to both philosophers and common people.

Through great struggle, Paul established churches all over the Mediterranean world. And to make sure these groups remained faithful to Jesus Christ, he wrote letters to them. These letters make up thirteen or fourteen of the New Testament books. (The authorship of Hebrews is not certain.)

Throughout his letters, Paul spoke from his authority as an apostle and repeatedly indicated that he had not been appointed to apostleship by any group of men, but by God himself. John R. Stott observes that "the word 'apostle' was not a general word which could be applied to every Christian like the words 'believer,' 'saint,' or 'brother.' It was a special term reserved for the Twelve and for one or two others whom the risen Christ had personally appointed" (*Only One Way,* p. 13. London: Inter-Varsity Press, 1968). Paul's call to be an apostle came from his personal encounter with the risen Christ on the Damascus road.

As we walk with Paul through the many struggles, challenges, and victories of his life's ministry, there is much we can learn about the life of a growing, purposeful Christian. Paul was a pioneer, blazing trails for many missionaries, pastors, and laypeople to come.

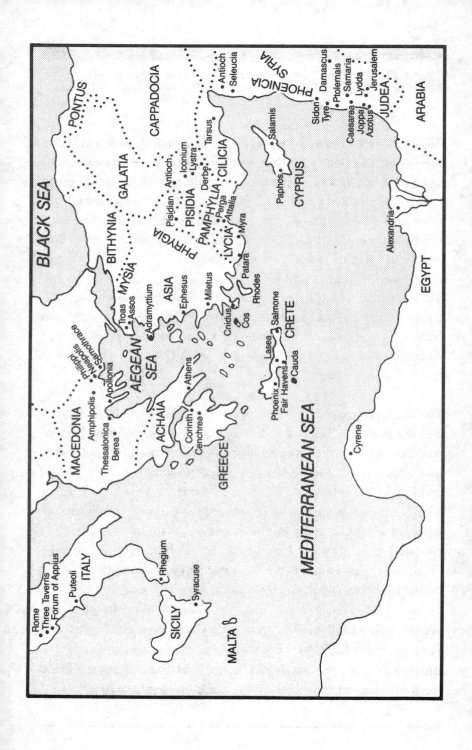

HOW TO USE THIS STUDYGUIDE

Fisherman studyguides are based on the inductive approach to Bible study. Inductive study is discovery study; we discover what the Bible says as we ask questions about its content and search for answers. This is quite different from the process in which a teacher *tells* a group *about* the Bible and what it means and what to do about it. In inductive study God speaks directly to each of us through his Word.

A group functions best when a leader keeps the discussion on target, but this leader is neither the teacher nor the "answer person." A leader's responsibility is to *ask*—not *tell*. The answers come from the text itself as group members examine, discuss, and think together about the passage.

There are four kinds of questions in each study. The first is an *approach question*. Used before the Bible passage is read, this question breaks the ice and helps you focus on the topic of the Bible study. It begins to reveal where thoughts and feelings need to be transformed by Scripture.

Some of the earlier questions in each study are *observation questions* designed to help you find out basic facts—who, what, where, when, and how.

When you know what the Bible says you need to ask, *What does it mean?* These *interpretation questions* help you to discover the writer's basic message.

Application questions ask, *What does it mean to me?* They challenge you to live out the Scripture's life-transforming message.

Fisherman studyguides provide spaces between questions for jotting down responses and related questions you would like to raise in the group. Each group member should have a copy of the studyguide and may take a turn in leading the group.

For consistency, Fisherman guides are written from the *New International Version.* But a group should feel free to use the NIV or any other accurate, modern translation of the Bible such as the *New Living Translation,* the *New Revised Standard Version,* the *New Jerusalem Bible,* or the *Good News Bible.* (Other paraphrases of the Bible may be referred to when additional help is needed.) Bible commentaries should not be brought to a Bible study because they tend to dampen discussion and keep people from thinking for themselves.

SUGGESTIONS FOR GROUP LEADERS

1. Read and study the Bible passage thoroughly beforehand, grasping its themes and applying its teachings for yourself. Pray that the Holy Spirit will "guide you into truth" so that your leadership will guide others.

2. If the studyguide's questions ever seem ambiguous or unnatural to you, rephrase them, feeling free to add others that seem necessary to bring out the meaning of a verse.

3. Begin (and end) the study promptly. Start by asking someone to pray for God's help. Remember, the Holy Spirit is the teacher, not you!

4. Ask for volunteers to read the passages out loud.

5. As you ask the studyguide's questions in sequence, encourage everyone to participate in the discussion. If some are silent, ask, "What do you think, Heather?" or, "Dan, what can you add to that answer?" or suggest, "Let's have an answer from someone who hasn't spoken up yet."

6. If a question comes up that you can't answer, don't be afraid to admit that you're baffled! Assign the topic as a research project for someone to report on next week.

7. Keep the discussion moving and focused. Though tangents will inevitably be introduced, you can bring the discussion back to the topic at hand. Learn to pace the discussion so that you finish a study each session you meet.

8. Don't be afraid of silences: some questions take time to answer and some people need time to gather courage to speak. If silence persists, rephrase your question, but resist the temptation to answer it yourself.

9. If someone comes up with an answer that is clearly illogical or unbiblical, ask him or her for further clarification: "What verse suggests that to you?"

10. Discourage Bible-hopping and overuse of cross-references. Learn all you can from *this* passage, along with a few important references suggested in the studyguide.

11. Some questions are marked with a ♦. This indicates that further information is available in the Leader's Notes at the back of the guide.

12. For further information on getting a new Bible study group started and keeping it functioning effectively, read Gladys Hunt's *You Can Start a Bible Study Group* and *Pilgrims in Progress: Growing through Groups* by Jim and Carol Plueddemann.

SUGGESTIONS FOR GROUP MEMBERS

1. Learn and apply the following ground rules for effective Bible study. (If new members join the group later, review these guidelines with the whole group.)

2. Remember that your goal is to learn all that you can *from the Bible passage being studied.* Let it speak for itself without using Bible commentaries or other Bible passages. There is more than enough in each assigned passage to keep your group productively occupied for one session. Sticking to the passage saves the group from insecurity and confusion.

3. Avoid the temptation to bring up those fascinating tangents that don't really grow out of the passage you are discussing. If the topic is of common interest, you can bring it up later in informal conversation following the study. Meanwhile, help each other stick to the subject!

4. Encourage each other to participate. People remember best what they discover and verbalize for themselves. Some people are naturally shyer than others, or they may be afraid of making a mistake. If your discussion is free and friendly and you show real interest in what other group members think and feel, they will be more likely to speak up. Remember, the more people involved in a discussion, the richer it will be.

5. Guard yourself from answering too many questions or talking too much. Give others a chance to express themselves. If you are one who participates easily, discipline yourself by counting to ten before you open your mouth!

6. Make personal, honest applications and commit yourself to letting God's Word change you.

SAUL MEETS JESUS

Acts 7:54–8:3; 9:1-31

Paul first appears as Saul, a zealous Pharisee and a great persecutor of Christians. He is briefly mentioned in the account of the disciple Stephen's death by stoning. We sense a callousness in Saul, but also a purposeful drive in his life. This same energy and drive is what God will later use for the purposes of Christ's kingdom.

1. If you can, relate a time when you have had an unmistakable encounter with God.

Read Acts 7:54–8:3.

2. What effect did Stephen's death seem to have on Saul?

Read Acts 9:1-19a.

3. What was still Saul's purpose (verses 1-2)? Read Acts
26:9-11 for Paul's own statement about the intensity of
his opposition to Christians.

4. What did Jesus tell Saul to do?

In harassing the Christians, who had Saul really been per-
secuting?

5. How did this encounter affect Saul physically? How
did it affect his traveling companions?

Why do you think Jesus chose to meet Saul in such a dramatic way?

6. How would you describe Ananias?

What job did the Lord assign him?

7. Why did Ananias hesitate, and what reassured him?

How did his obedience demonstrate his faith?

◆ **8.** What was Saul's attitude as he waited to hear from God?

In your own words, describe what happened to him when he met Ananias.

9. Saul had erected a barrier of hostility against Christians. Ananias had a wall of fear. How did Jesus Christ remove both barriers?

What kinds of walls do we build between ourselves and others?

Read Acts 9:19b-31.

10. Contrast Saul in 9:1 with Saul in verses 20-22, 27.
Why would preaching in the synagogue demand courage?

How did Saul identify Jesus to the people?

11. How disturbing was Saul's preaching to the Jews
(verses 23-24, 29)?

Why do you think God's purposes for Saul included suf-
fering (go back to 9:16)?

12. Why were the Jerusalem believers hesitant to accept Saul?

Suppose your father or son had been one of those previously seized by Saul, imprisoned, and perhaps put to death. How would you feel if Saul wanted to join your fellowship of Christians?

◆ **13.** Describe the part Barnabas played in this situation.

14. Read the summary statement made about the church in verse 31. How successful had its enemies been in stamping out Christianity?

What does this mean to you as a Christian in today's world?

GOD CALLS PAUL AND BARNABAS

Acts 13

Though many Christians know the relief of finding peace with God and new life in Christ, often they don't learn the next step: *calling*. This is the process by which God shows us what we are to do with our lives, now that we are his. We can have many callings in a lifetime, as situations change and God gives direction. Paul's first calling was unmistakable.

1. Do you remember ever being "called" by God to do something? Explain briefly.

Read Acts 13:1-12.

2. Briefly describe the spiritual climate of the church in Antioch (verses 1-3; see also Acts 11:21-26).

What was the Holy Spirit's special message to the believers?

3. Though the Antioch church was sending them, who was actually calling Barnabas and Saul to this work (verses 2, 4)?

Where did they go? Follow their journey on the map on page 6. (Cyprus happened to be Barnabas's home country.)

◆ **11.** Why did the word of the Lord spread so rapidly?

In this situation, how did the Jews show their opposition?

12. Review this chapter and notice four ways in which the Holy Spirit worked (verses 2, 4, 9, 52). Have you experienced the Holy Spirit at work in your life or church in any of these ways?

PREACHING AND PERSECUTION

Acts 14

It is a simple matter to hold opinions. It is much more difficult to speak out with authority, knowing that what you are saying is strange—and in some cases objectionable—to your hearers. Fortunately, Paul already had a history of living by his convictions. He had been a good Pharisee, trained in Jewish law, and he was determined to carry it out even if it meant killing people. Now Paul did not carry the authority of the religious community, but he did carry God's authority to speak of Jesus. And he found the tables turned upon him.

1. When is it most difficult for you to speak out for Christian values?

Read Acts 14:1-7.

2. In what ways were the apostles' ministry and experience in Iconium similar to that of Pisidian Antioch?

3. What was the tactic of the unbelieving Jews (verse 2)?

How did the apostles show they were not intimidated, and how did God back them up?

4. Why did the apostles flee to Lystra and Derbe?

What did they keep doing as they traveled?

Read Acts 14:8-18.

5. Besides physical need, what more did Paul see in the crippled man?

♦ 6. How did the crowds respond to the miracle?

With what frantic action and message did Paul and Barnabas try to stop the people's response?

7. How might any pagan people, such as these who did not have the Old Testament Scriptures, become aware of the true God?

Read Acts 14:19-28.

8. Why did the people of Lystra completely reverse their attitude toward Paul and Barnabas?

Why do you think they could not kill Paul?

9. Why do you think Paul and Barnabas returned to the places where they had been mistreated?

10. What follow-up program did they use to insure that the work would continue (verses 21-23)?

11. Their prayers were often accompanied by fasting (see Acts 13:2-3). What do you think fasting accomplishes, and why?

12. Why did Paul and Barnabas return to Antioch?

What did they emphasize in their report?

13. What do you think were the highlights of this first missionary journey?

14. Review the ways God used Paul and Barnabas and helped them. How do these things challenge and encourage you?

PAUL CONFRONTS LEGALISM

Acts 15

Although all of us complain about rules, we depend upon them for order and security. Rules eliminate the need for us to make complex choices. Rules stay the same. When we follow the rules, the system works for us—or so we are told. But once we become alive to God's Spirit, we find that mere rules fall short of providing fulfillment. Rules may give us guidance—but they don't change our hearts. Real, inner change happens only as we learn to listen to and follow the Holy Spirit.

As a former Pharisee, Paul knew all about rules. As a Christian leader, he now had to turn his back on an old security system—and lead others in understanding the new "rule" of love.

1. When have rules been good for you? When have they not been so good?

Read Acts 15:1-21.

2. What point of dispute comes between Paul and Barnabas and some men from Judea and Antioch?

♦ **3.** How serious was this conflict to Paul, and what did he and Barnabas do about it?

4. How were Paul and Barnabas received by the church in Jerusalem?

What did they emphasize in their report to the church (verse 4)?

5. Who gathered to discuss the issue of circumcision and other Jewish laws?

Scanning through this passage, what do you perceive to be the general atmosphere of this debate?

6. Who addressed the assembly, and what were the arguments presented for accepting Gentiles into the fellowship (verses 1-18)?

7. According to verse 11, what was the central issue?

What legalistic demands do some people still insist on today for full salvation?

♦ **8.** Why do you think James offered the concluding guidelines he does in verse 20?

Read Acts 15:22-35.

9. Describe the people who joined Paul and Barnabas on their return trip to Antioch. What was their mission?

10. What part did the Holy Spirit have in the decision reached by the church (verse 28)?

How did the believers in Antioch receive the news?

11. From this experience of the early church, what can we learn about problem solving?

Read Acts 15:36-41.

12. This next trip marks the beginning of the second missionary journey. What was Paul's motivation for another trip?

◆ **13.** Describe the conflict that arose between Paul and Barnabas as they made plans.

What resulted from the disagreement?

14. What has impressed you most about this part of Paul's story? Why?

PRAISING IN PRISON

Acts 16

When we follow Christ's path, we often end up in strange places. And we usually don't know how things are going to turn out. When Paul's ministry landed him in prison, he had no New Testament to turn to for encouragement, to see what others had done before him. He didn't know what the end of his story would be. This makes his ability to praise God in difficult circumstances even more astonishing.

1. Mention a time when you unexpectedly found joy in the midst of a bad situation.

Read Acts 16:1-10.

◆ **2.** What do we learn about Timothy here?

Why would he be an asset to Paul's missionary team?

3. What message did the three carry to the churches?

What were the continued results of their visits?

4. What role did the Holy Spirit play in Paul's planning?

Who apparently needed special help at this time?

Read Acts 16:11-15.

◆ **5.** Check the party's route on the map. Why was Philippi chosen as a starting point for their ministry in Macedonia?

6. Since there was apparently no synagogue in the city, what did Paul go looking for on the Sabbath?

7. Why would Lydia be a significant convert?

Read Acts 16:16-40.

Assign one person to read the narration, and others for each of the spoken parts: the slave girl, Paul, the girl's owners, and the jailer.

8. According to verse 16, in what two ways was the life of this girl bound?

9. What did the spirit in the slave girl recognize about Paul and his party?

How did Paul deal with the spirit?

10. How did the girl's deliverance affect her owners, and the crowd?

11. Physically, Paul and Silas were prisoners, yet how did they express their freedom?

Do you think you could respond in this way? Why or why not?

12. Summarize the events that night in the jail. What change occurred in the lives of the jailer and his family members?

13. What dilemma faced the officials the next day, and how did they resolve it?

14. If someone were to ask you, "What must I do to be saved?" how would you answer? Would you be speaking from theory or personal experience?

PAUL THE PHILOSOPHER

Acts 17

It's not always easy to know how to communicate with others. Differences in family background, culture, and experience make each person a mystery. One key to sharing God's love with others is to learn early on about the person you are talking to.

With all the traveling he did and the variety of people he met, Paul had to become an expert in "reading" people. Consequently, we find several different explanations of God's love in Paul's encounters with people. He explained this to Jews using their own law and history. Or, as in the case of this passage, he tapped into the surrounding culture for clues to make the true God known.

1. What picture or symbol explaining God's love is most meaningful to you, and why?

Read Acts 17:1-15.

2. What was Paul's pattern of preaching and the content of his message (verses 2-3)?

Who was convinced by the force of the truth?

3. Why did the unbelieving Jews incite a riot?

What unintentional compliment did they give the disciples, and what falsehood did they spread (verses 6-7)?

◆ **4.** With what was Jason charged? How did the city authorities handle the case?

5. Who became hostile and why (verse 13)?

What role did Paul's brothers in Christ play both in Thessalonica and Berea (verses 10, 14)?

Read Acts 17:16-34.

6. What bothered Paul about Athens? What bothered the philosophers about Paul?

◆ **7.** What did Paul emphasize in his preaching?

What common ground did he establish with his listeners?

8. How did Paul describe God and his relationship to humankind (verses 24-25)?

How had the Athenians groped for God?

♦ **9.** How near is God to every person (verses 27-28)?

If God is so near in his involvement with people all through history, why do you think people have missed him?

10. What forms of idolatry do people engage in today?

Why do people want to worship something less than the true and living God?

♦ **11.** Why do people need to repent?

12. Who is going to judge all humankind? What credentials does this judge have?

13. In what three ways did the Athenians react to Paul's message?

How do people today display these same responses?

CRISIS IN CORINTH

Acts 18

Paul's life is certainly proof that becoming a Christian does not end our troubles; in fact, trouble seemed to follow this apostle. But God gave Paul specific assurances, and Paul had the opportunity to learn the value of lasting friendships.

1. What helps you cope when you face difficult times?

◆ **Read Acts 18:1-17.**

2. What did Paul's new friends have in common with him? Why were they in Corinth?

Why would Paul need friends like these?

3. What did Paul do every week? When Silas and Timothy arrived?

4. What was his message to the Jewish Corinthians?

5. How did Paul respond to the opposition that developed (see also Acts 13:51)?

Considering the opposition of verse 6, what did Crispus's faith demonstrate?

6. In what special way did the Lord encourage Paul?

What evidence is there that the Lord kept his word (verse 11)?

7. What is your impression of Gallio, the proconsul (verses 12-17)?

8. What had apparently happened to Crispus, Sosthenes' predecessor?

How was God keeping his promise of verse 10?

9. If you were in a difficult situation, such as Paul's, what kind of help could you expect from the Lord?

Read Acts 18:18-28.

(Note that verse 23 describes the beginning of Paul's third missionary journey.)

◆ **10.** Following Paul's progress on the map, list the activities and the decisions recorded in verses 18-23.

What was of first importance to Paul in the plans he made (verse 21)?

11. Discuss Apollos's character, listing all the descriptive phrases used of him in this passage.

12. In what area was he weak?

How did Priscilla and Aquila help him?

13. What can we learn from this couple about ministry and Christian fellowship?

PAUL IN EPHESUS

Acts 19

There is much pressure in our world today to be accepting of others' religious beliefs, sexual orientations, and civil rights. When tolerance is the rule of the day, the gospel's claim to truth is misunderstood and often maligned. Paul experienced some of the same opposition in Ephesus. When Paul's persuasive teaching began to offend people, there was quite a stir.

1. What kinds of opposition do Christians meet when they proclaim Christ's message in a society filled with other religions?

◆ **Read Acts 19:1-20.**

2. What deficiency did Paul find in the disciples at Ephesus? What did he do?

◆ **3.** Describe the baptism of John. How was it incomplete?

4. What verbs are used in verse 8 to describe how Paul presented the gospel? What words describe some of the hearers in verse 9?

Can you think of present-day examples in which the terms in these verses could be used to describe those who share the gospel message and those who reject it?

5. How successful was the opposition (verse 10)?

6. What did God do to help the sick and oppressed through Paul (verses 11-12)?

As a result of what God was doing, what counterfeit activity began?

7. How was the counterfeit exposed and its work stopped?

What was necessary besides the use of the name of Jesus to cast out evil spirits?

8. How did this episode affect:

the community's view of the Lord Jesus?

those who had become believers?

the ministry, as believers were cleansed from evil practices?

9. What kind of evil supernatural operations do we see today?

How can believers still be caught up in the practice of magical arts?

Read Acts 19:21-41.

10. As his work in Ephesus drew to a close, what travel plans did Paul make (verse 21)? Trace his proposed journey on the map.

11. In what way was Christianity affecting both the religious practice and the economy in Ephesus (verses 26-27)?

12. What was the basis for the agitation started by Demetrius? What do we see about mob psychology from this riot?

◆ **13.** How was order finally restored?

A FAREWELL MESSAGE

Acts 20

An exciting aspect of ministry is the great adventure of meeting new people in many different settings. One of the heartbreaks is having to say good-bye to those who have become an integral part of your life and ministry. Paul worked hard as a spiritual leader, pouring himself into the lives of Christians in each place. It must have been difficult for him to carry so many people in his heart and prayers. It is not surprising that he takes great care to instruct them before he leaves.

1. How many Christians around the country (or world) do you communicate with regularly? What is difficult and rewarding about this?

Read Acts 20:1-12.

2. On what day and for what purpose were the believers in Troas gathered (verse 7)?

Describe their meeting place. Why do you suppose they met at night?

3. What dramatic incident occurred?

Read Acts 20:13-38.

◆ **4.** How had Paul conducted himself in Ephesus, in regard to:

his outreach?

his enemies?

his message (verses 20-21)?

5. What part did the Holy Spirit play in Paul's ministry and plans (verses 22-23, 28)?

What are some ways the Holy Spirit has "warned" you?

6. What was Paul's life purpose, and how did it affect the way he valued his own life?

7. Why was Paul's conscience clear (verses 20, 26-27, 31)?

8. How would the church elders need to respond to Paul's charge and warning (verses 28-32, 35)?

PAUL'S ARREST

Acts 21

As a former Pharisee, Paul knew perhaps better than anyone what a radical message he was proclaiming. There was no comfortable ground; Jews rejected Jesus, and pagans resented the effect Christianity had on their idol worship. Paul was bound for trouble as long as he remained true to preaching Jesus Christ crucified and risen again.

1. What conflicts do you have in your life, simply because you are a Christian?

Read Acts 21:1-16.

2. What kind of bond was established with the Christians in Tyre after only a week with them?

◆ **3.** Who was Philip (verse 8)? How were his children involved in his ministry (verse 9)?

◆ **4.** How did Paul respond to the prophecy of Agabus?

What attitude had Paul previously declared (Acts 20:22-24)?

5. How did the believers receive Paul's decision?

Share some specific ways we are called on to accept God's will for ourselves and also for other believers.

Read Acts 21:17-40.

6. What did Paul emphasize in his report to the elders in Jerusalem?

How was the report received?

◆ 7. What false impression about Paul were the elders anxious to correct? What visible solution did they suggest?

8. How did Paul's actions get him into trouble with his Jewish enemies?

9. What did the crowd try to do to Paul? How was he rescued?

10. What surprised the officer in charge when Paul spoke to him?

What had he wrongly assumed about Paul?

11. Why do you think Paul requested to speak to the crowd?

Could you have done this? Why or why not?

12. In this chapter we see Paul move from the warm fellowship of Christian friends and followers to be the target of the murderous hostility of the Jerusalem Jews. His motive was obedience to the Holy Spirit. Examine your own loyalty to Jesus. How deep is it?

To what lengths would your obedience and faithfulness to God take you?

A PLOT TO KILL PAUL

Acts 22–23

People grow passionate when something in which they are deeply invested is challenged. We feel strongly about our religious beliefs, our political system, even the traditions we were trained to reverence. In this episode of Paul's life, he challenges the Jewish religious leaders, and—not surprisingly—incites violent anger.

1. Have you ever had to change your position on some important matter? Describe how that process felt to you.

Read Acts 22:1-21.

2. Besides speaking in their language, what did Paul tell his Jewish audience to show them how much he had in common with them?

Why would the mention of Gamaliel be significant? (See Acts 5:34.)

3. Review Paul's conversion given in Acts 9. What further personal facts did he relate here?

What did he emphasize as the purpose for his conversion (verses 14-15)?

4. Of all his experiences, Paul chose to tell about his conversion when witnessing to the Jews. What factors in your conversion experience (whether dramatic or not) could you share with others to communicate the reality of your faith in Jesus Christ?

Read Acts 22:22-30.

5. Why did the crowd cut short Paul's message?

How was the Roman official going to investigate Paul?

6. What right had been denied to Paul as a Roman citizen?

Think of examples today where the laws of the land protect Christians.

Read Acts 23:1-11.

7. What claim did Paul make as he began his defense before the Sanhedrin?

Why would the high priest object to Paul's statement?

♦ 8. Discuss the exchange between Paul and the high priest. Why would Paul make such strong statements?

What do we learn about Paul's attitude toward authority?

9. What were the doctrinal differences in the council, and how did Paul use them to his advantage?

10. What happened to encourage Paul in all of this (verse 11)?

Read Acts 23:12-35.

11. How deep was the Jews' hatred of Paul? Give evidence for your answer.

How were the priests and elders as guilty as the conspirators?

12. Who were the key figures in Paul's rescue?

How far was the commander willing to go to protect this Roman citizen?

13. In what ways was God at work in Paul's life in this chapter?

14. What risks might the Lord ask you to take for him?

How does Paul's experience encourage you to know God will help you in these situations?

THE TRIAL BEFORE FELIX AND FESTUS

Acts 24–25

People—even great leaders and important dignitaries—who have not been spiritually reborn cannot understand spiritual matters. Paul's appearances before Felix and Festus illustrate this truth well. These leaders are caught up in politics, trying to keep the Jews happy. Yet the Jews keep bringing up this strange case—and they are very adamant!

1. How are matters of the spirit—religious faith—usually approached by political figures? Give examples if you can.

Read Acts 24.

2. Picture this dramatic courtroom scene. What specific charges did Tertullus bring against Paul?

3. Contrast the opening remarks of Tertullus and Paul. In his own defense what admission did Paul make?

4. What did he have in common with his accusers (verses 14-15)?

5. What weakness did Paul point out in the prosecution's case (verse 19)?

◆ **6.** What did Paul speak to Felix and his wife about? How did Felix respond?

7. What reasons or excuses do people give today for not committing themselves to Jesus and his message?

Read Acts 25:1-12.

8. What was still lacking in the accusations before Festus (verse 7)?

What advantage might the Jews have hoped to gain by approaching Festus right after he took office (verse 9)?

9. Why did Paul refuse to go to Jerusalem for trial? What appeal did he make?

Read Acts 25:13-27.

10. What had Festus discovered about the dispute between Paul and his accusers?

♦ **11.** Why do you think Paul's case interested Agrippa? How important had this case become?

12. What is your impression of Paul's character revealed throughout these proceedings?

PAUL BEFORE AGRIPPA

Acts 26

Paul's experiences are proof of the importance for Christians to have a clear understanding of what they believe and why. He was a mystery to the authorities who took him into custody. They had trouble understanding why this single man was causing such a commotion. It was the perfect opportunity for Paul to give a detailed testimony. He had their undivided attention. And he was careful to give a full account of God's grace in his life.

1. Have you had a public opportunity to give testimony to Christ's work in your life? Describe briefly.

Read Acts 26:1-23.

2. How did Paul describe his early life to Agrippa?

What did good Pharisees believe? (See Acts 23:8.)

3. For what basic issue was Paul standing trial (verses 6-8)?

♦ 4. What is the "hope" he described in verses 6-7?

If you were a Pharisee or an Old Testament scholar, how would you answer Paul's question in verse 8?

5. As a Pharisee, what had been Paul's reaction to Jesus and the Way?

When Jesus met him personally, what became clear to Paul?

6. Using verses 16-18, describe God's purpose for Paul, his message, and the results for those who believed.

7. What was the condition of the unbelievers described in verse 18?

How do you think his current audience liked being described in these terms?

8. Does Paul's description still fit unbelievers? Explain.

What kind of transformation can faith in the risen Christ produce in people today?

9. What message applied to both Jew and Gentile (verse 20)?

Why would the Jews be so hostile toward Paul?

10. Who was Paul's support (verse 22)?

What similar help and support does the believer receive today? (See Acts 1:8 and Romans 15:4.)

Read Acts 26:24-32.

11. Why would Festus think Paul was irrational?

12. Into what dilemma was Agrippa placed by Paul's comments and question, and how did he deal with the issue?

Of what had Paul convinced both Festus and Agrippa?

13. In what ways was Paul's missionary heart revealed in this passage?

THE STORM AND SHIPWRECK

Acts 27

All of us go through crises, but we don't always see them as opportunities for God to reveal himself to others. Paul's presence on an ill-fated ship made a difference in the lives of many people. Paul did not see himself as special, but his God as faithful.

1. How do you usually react to a crisis? Would you like to have a different response? If so, explain.

Read Acts 27:1-26.

2. Trace Paul's sea voyage on the map. What friends were traveling with Paul? What hindered their rapid progress (verses 4, 7-8)?

♦ **3.** Paul, a seasoned traveler, offered what advice?

What influenced the centurion's decision not to stay where they were safe (verses 11-13)?

♦ **4.** List all the factors that made their situation desperate (verses 14-20). (Note the descriptive adjectives and verbs.)

How deep was their despair?

5. After saying "I told you so," how did Paul encourage his fellow travelers?

How could he be so confident?

6. What promise to Paul was God keeping (Acts 23:11)?

How would others benefit from God's will being performed in Paul's life?

7. How was this crisis situation a test of Paul's faith?

8. Think of your answer to question 1, and the emergencies and crises you have experienced in your own life. How did your response in these situations compare with Paul's?

9. What can all of us learn about faith from Paul's example?

Read Acts 27:27-44.

10. What physical problems did they still face?

11. How did Paul's status change during the course of the voyage?

12. How did Paul again encourage and help his shipmates?

How did God keep his promise to each of them?

13. How have other Christian believers helped you in crisis situations? Thank God for them!

PAUL ARRIVES IN ROME

Acts 28

According to tradition, Paul was martyred in Rome, although no one is sure of the year or even the circumstances. He probably guessed as he traveled that he was journeying ultimately to his own death. Yet his purposes remained steadfast, and he did not slow his pace, except to stay with believers to teach and encourage. His life is an example to us of faithful commitment and the relinquishment of personal dreams and ambitions.

1. How would you state your life purpose?

Read Acts 28:1-10.

2. Find Malta on the map to see how far the ship had been driven. Why was it a good place to be shipwrecked?

3. What did the natives assume about Paul when he was bitten by the snake? To what extent did they change their minds?

♦ **4.** Paul had just spent weeks at sea. How did God encourage and prepare him now for Rome?

What miracles was God still working through Paul?

5. Review briefly the obstacles Paul had faced since he set out for Rome in Acts 19:21. How long did it take? (See Acts 20:3; 21:4; 24:27; 27:41; 28:11.)

6. What can we learn from Paul about endurance, faith, courage, patience, and hope as we head toward God's goals for us in our own lives and experience?

Read Acts 28:11-31.

7. What did Paul do when he reached Rome (verses 14-17)?

8. Why did Paul summon the Jewish leaders?

9. What might Paul have expected these Roman Jews to have heard about him? How did he set the record straight?

10. What was the "hope of Israel" (verse 20)? (See also Acts 26:6-8.) How central was this to Paul's message?

11. How did the response of the Jews in Rome to Isaiah's prophecy typify Jewish response throughout Paul's ministry? Find other examples of this in Acts.

For Review

12. Think through the highlights of Paul's life and ministry. How was Christ's commission given in Acts 1:8 fulfilled through him?

How do we know that God's Good News is for everyone, Jew or Gentile?

13. What words did Paul use in his teaching to describe the transaction of becoming related to God through Christ?

14. God moved powerfully in the pagan world of Paul's day. How is God at work today?

What changes have occurred in your life as you studied Acts?

LEADER'S NOTES

Study 1/Saul Meets Jesus

Question 8. After this experience, Saul apparently spent three years in Arabia (Galatians 1:15-18). Exactly when Saul left for Arabia is not clear. However, shortly after his conversion he went away to spend time alone with God.

Question 13. In Acts 4:36 we find that *Barnabas* means "Son of Encouragement."

Study 2/God Calls Paul and Barnabas

Question 6. Paul's sermon is representative of the sermons he preached in the synagogues he visited, where his audiences were primarily people who knew the Old Testament Scriptures.

Question 11. As the gospel spread, the Jews generally rejected the message and the Gentiles received it. This became the pattern in the missionary journeys.

◼ Study 3/Preaching and Persecution

Question 6. When Paul and Barnabas tore their clothes, they were exhibiting a Jewish sign of horror over the possibility of blasphemy.

◼ Study 4/Paul Confronts Legalism

Question 3. Sometime during the next week, read the epistle to the Galatians to understand the seriousness of this problem, which had arisen in the churches in Galatia as well as in Antioch.

Question 8. Although the leaders in Jerusalem were struggling over the issue of circumcision, they decided not to require this rite of Gentile believers. Rather, they were concerned about Christian lifestyle, which meant disassociation from idols and attention to sexual purity.

Question 13. Later Paul reevaluated John Mark's effectiveness (2 Timothy 4:11).

◼ Study 5/Praising in Prison

Question 2. Timothy's circumcision was an act of expediency because Timothy was half Jewish. Paul did not demand this of a full Gentile.

Question 5. From the pronoun *we,* beginning in Acts 16:10, it appears that the writer of Acts (thought by many scholars to be Luke) joined Paul's party.

■ Study 6/Paul the Philosopher

Question 4. In Acts we see many examples of Christians relating to political authorities. The writer is careful in each instance to state objectively what happens. The Christian disciples were sometimes accused of sedition, but political activism was not their purpose.

Question 7. "Eat, drink, and be merry, for tomorrow we die" was the Epicureans' philosophy, whereas the Stoics refused to submit to either pleasure or pain. The Areopagus was a court in which matters of religion, philosophy, and morals were discussed. It was not a trial court; it was more an open forum.

Question 9. For more insight on this question, read Romans 1:19-25.

Question 11. Repentance as it is taught in the New Testament includes: an admission of guilt—"I have done wrong," genuine contrition—"I am sorry for my sin," and a commitment to a new way of life—"From now on I want to live to please God."

■ Study 7/Crisis in Corinth

Note on Acts 18. Corinth was the capital of the Roman province of Achaia. It was a flourishing commercial city, a center for both land and sea trade. It was known for its cosmopolitan citizens, and it had a reputation for corrupt religious and immoral practices. Paul later wrote two significant letters to the believers established in Corinth. For a "before and after" description, read 1 Corinthians 6:9-11.

Question 10. The kind of vow Paul took in Acts 18:18 is not stated, but it has been speculated that he had taken a temporary Nazirite vow (part of which was not cutting one's hair) in thanksgiving to God for his protection in Corinth.

Study 8/Paul in Ephesus

Note on Acts 19. Ephesus was a wealthy, important city in Asia Minor. It was a stronghold for pagan practices of superstition and the magical arts. The center of worship was the Temple of Artemis, one of the seven wonders of the world. Because it was an important population center, Paul stayed there about three years and built up the work begun by other believers.

Question 3. See Mark 1:4-5, 8, for more background on John's baptism.

Question 13. The leading citizens were friendly to Paul and concerned about his safety. The city clerk called for legal action, not mob rule. These factors show us again that Christianity was accepted as a religion and protected by law.

Study 9/A Farewell Message

Question 4. Paul's message in Acts 20:18-35 is particularly important because it was directed to a Christian audience, specifically to church leaders. In it he spoke of his example as a leader, his future, and his charge and benediction to the leaders.

Study 10/Paul's Arrest

Question 3. Read Acts 6:1-6; 8:4-8 for more background about Philip.

Question 4. Read Mark 10:32-34 and Luke 22:42 and compare Jesus' experience with Paul's.

Question 7. These four men had apparently taken a Nazirite vow and their time of purification was almost up. The church leaders felt that if Paul was seen taking part in this Jewish custom, then he could effectively quell the rumors about Paul's turning people against the Law. Many have criticized Paul for what he did, seeing it as a compromise, but the principle of being all things to all people in 1 Corinthians 9:19-23 may explain his decision.

■ Study 11/A Plot to Kill Paul

Question 8. Paul may not have recognized the high priest because (a) he may not have been wearing the robes of his office, (b) Paul could not see who had spoken, or (c) he would not expect such an action from the high priest.

■ Study 12/The Trial Before Felix and Festus

Question 6. Drusilla was the daughter of the Herod mentioned in Acts 12.

Question 11. Agrippa was the son of Herod (see Acts 12) and was known to be an expert in Jewish affairs. Festus, a Roman, welcomed his counsel on this problem with Paul.

■ Study 13/Paul Before Agrippa

Question 4. See Job 19:25-26, Isaiah 26:19, and Daniel 12:2 for some Old Testament previews of this hope.

■ Study 14/The Storm and Shipwreck

Question 3. The Fast referred to in Acts 27:9 was the Jewish fast for the Day of Atonement. This occurred around October 5 in A.D. 59. Sailing became dangerous after mid-September and impossible after mid-November because of winter storms.

Question 4. Remember that sighting the sun and stars was essential for navigation in those days.

■ Study 15/Paul Arrives in Rome

Question 4. The word *healed* in Acts 28:8 describes a miraculous cure. The word *cured* used in Acts 28:9 can also be translated "treated," which would imply medical treatment. Remember that Luke, Paul's companion, was a physician.

WHAT SHOULD WE STUDY NEXT?

To help your group answer that question, we've listed the Fisherman Guides by category so you can choose your next study.

TOPICAL STUDIES

Angels, Wright

Becoming Women of Purpose, Barton

Building Your House on the Lord, Brestin

Discipleship, Reapsome

Doing Justice, Showing Mercy, Wright

Encouraging Others, Johnson

Examining the Claims of Jesus, Brestin

Friendship, Brestin

The Fruit of the Spirit, Briscoe

Great Doctrines of the Bible, Board

Great Passages of the Bible, Plueddemann

Great Prayers of the Bible, Plueddemann

Growing Through Life's Challenges, Reapsome

Guidance & God's Will, Stark

Heart Renewal, Goring

Higher Ground, Brestin

Lifestyle Priorities, White

Marriage, Stevens

Miracles, Castleman

Moneywise, Larsen

One Body, One Spirit, Larsen

The Parables of Jesus, Hunt

Prayer, Jones

The Prophets, Wright

Proverbs & Parables, Brestin

Satisfying Work, Stevens & Schoberg

Senior Saints, Reapsome

Sermon on the Mount, Hunt

Spiritual Warfare, Moreau

The Ten Commandments, Briscoe

Who Is God? Seemuth

Who Is the Holy Spirit? Knuckles & Van Reken

Who Is Jesus? Van Reken

Witnesses to All the World, Plueddemann

Worship, Sibley

BIBLE BOOK STUDIES

Genesis, Fromer & Keyes

Job, Klug

Psalms, Klug

Proverbs: Wisdom That Works, Wright

Ecclesiastes, Brestin

Jonah, Habakkuk, & Malachi, Fromer & Keyes

Matthew, Sibley

Mark, Christensen

Luke, Keyes

John: Living Word, Kuniholm

Acts 1-12, Christensen

Paul (Acts 13-28), Christensen

Romans: The Christian Story, Reapsome

1 Corinthians, Hummel

Strengthened to Serve (2 Corinthians), Plueddemann

Galatians, Titus & Philemon, Kuniholm

Ephesians, Baylis

Philippians, Klug

Colossians, Shaw

Letters to the Thessalonians, Fromer & Keyes

Letters to Timothy, Fromer & Keyes

Hebrews, Hunt

James, Christensen

1 & 2 Peter, Jude, Brestin

How Should a Christian Live? (1, 2 & 3 John), Brestin

Revelation, Hunt

BIBLE CHARACTER STUDIES

David: Man after God's Own Heart, Castleman

Elijah, Castleman

Great People of the Bible, Plueddemann

King David: Trusting God for a Lifetime, Castleman

Men Like Us, Heidebrecht & Scheuermann

Paul (Acts 13-28), Christensen

Peter, Castleman

Ruth & Daniel, Stokes

Women Like Us, Barton

Women Who Achieved for God, Christensen

Women Who Believed God, Christensen